Growing Up With Relatives

Dad's Side

Don Wadley

YorkshirePublishing
www.yorkshirepublishing.com
Write Now

Yorkshire Publishing
4613 E. 91st St.
Tulsa, Oklahoma 74137
www.YorkshirePublishing.com
918.394.2665

In the Beginning

It was a hot summer day in 1952. Working on a construction crew, I was excited about my first job. I was three years old. I remember pushing a little wooden, custom-made wheelbarrow with a wooden wheel around the framework of our new house. It was summer, and I was wearing a cool, stylish outfit my mom, born Alma Reva Spears, made for me from a piece of light colored material. She was quite a seamstress and not only made her own but clothes for the rest of the family also. Dad, my older brother Jim, and I were working to get the framing finished and the roof on before it rained. Grandma Wadley's brother, my dad's uncle, Oscar, was helping us with the construction. He was a home builder so I guess he was the boss. Uncle Oscar was a big, strong guy who laughed a lot and wore a straw hat to protect his shiny bald head.

House building is much faster and easier if you use power tools, but we didn't have any. All of the sawing and nailing was done with a hand saw and a hammer. I didn't know anything about building a house at my age, but I did know my assignment. Uncle Oscar made my wheelbarrow for me and made sure it was the correct size so I could handle it. He said, "Now Donnie Wayne, you push this thing around the job site and pick up all of the scrap pieces of wood." I was really proud of myself as I carefully dumped each load onto a pile of discarded lumber. After I finished that assignment, I was given another. Dad handed me a little short stick with a magnet on the end. My new job was to pick up nails that had been accidentally dropped and put them in a Folgers coffee can. I was a happy camper. That magnet stick was the coolest thing. The nails on the ground would jump up to the magnet and make a "clink" sound. I also found some other metal stuff: pop bottle caps and an old rusty butter knife.

A few weeks later, after the drywall was installed and the popcorn ceiling completed, Mom couldn't wait to paint the interior and hang a little wallpaper. She loved to paint and decorate. The house was a two bedroom with only one bathroom with a tub and no shower. My brother and I shared the same bed and never thought anything about it. I was just glad to have a nice, soft bed to sleep on. We would open our east window at night and listen to the clapping leaves of a big Silver Leaf Maple tree in the back yard. Train tracks were a couple of miles away and the train would blow its deep toned whistle about 10:00 every night as it railed North. We had a Phillips 66 refinery in town back in those days, and the train was probably loaded with fuel and headed for a distribution center.

Dad worked outside most of the time and usually got pretty dirty. He wanted a place where he could clean up without coming into the house, so he just built his own shower outside behind his shop. He poured a concrete slab and enclosed it with metal walls and a beefed up flat roof. The roof supported a black, 55 gallon drum filled with water. Dad made a long water gauge that he attached vertically to the outside of the drum so you could tell where the water level was. A shower head with a control handle came through the ceiling. Add a soap tray and towel hook and there you go. Just fill it up with the garden hose once a week or so and we were in business. That shower felt really good on hot summer days. There was an iron pipe fence next to the backside of the shower and for fun I would climb the fence, pull myself up onto the top of the shower and jump off. I tied a pillowcase to my back for a cape and pretended that I was Superman. I never flew an inch but did manage to screw my back up. I jumped out of the barn loft doorway one time and just about broke my neck. I don't recommend that, either. My mom was constantly telling me to stop jumping off things, but I just knew that one day I would fly. We had an iron swing set in the back yard that Dad made. It was very tall and chains connected the wooden seats to the top. You could pump yourself back and forth and get way up in the air and then let go and jump out, flying for approximately two seconds, although it seemed much longer. Now that was fun. I continued to propel myself from high objects and couldn't figure out why my back always hurt. As it turned out, Mom was right.

Our house sat on a couple of acres Dad purchased from Mr. Pollard. It was out in the country and I was fortunate to have my grandparents living close to us. They weren't just any grandparents. They were the best. I don't recall them ever getting upset or worrying about anything. It didn't matter what came their way, they never complained. The family Bible was actually read. Every day, Grandma would sit in the swing on her front porch, eat an apple and read a chapter or two. Grandpa would usually work in his big garden and talk with Mr. Montgomery, who lived across the road. An odd character, he had white hair and a white beard with trails of tobacco juice cascading down each side of his mouth and spoke with a thick accent. Grandpa didn't seem to have any trouble, but I never understood a word he said. His wife looked pretty much like him.

My Best Friend

Grandpa had two dogs and a half dozen cats. The field mice liked to congregate and make their little mice nests in the chicken house and barn because that's where all of the free food was stored. All they had to do was show up and eat grain. There was no mouse registration, no sign up sheet, not even a line to stand in, just come and dine on someone else's dime. What a deal!

Without cats the place would be overrun with mooching mice. That's why they're such an asset to any livestock operation. They know how to catch the furry little critters, preferring to hunt in teams. I used to watch them hop up on top of a feed barrel that was close to a known mouse trail and there they would wait. It wouldn't be long before they would crouch down and then leap off the barrel with claws extended. They would prance around with the prize in their mouth and then play with it for a few minutes before the final chomp to the neck. The cats never could wipe them all out because they reproduced at such a rapid rate.

When Grandpa was caught up on his work he would take time to grab his cane pole and walk down to Miss Pollard's pond to catch a few fish. The pesky grasshoppers were plentiful in the summer time, so they were used as bait. Catfish and perch love a crunchy grasshopper.

During the cold months, worms were the bait of choice. When the ground was too hard to dig up with a shovel it was time for the heavy artillery. My Dad liked to make unique tools for use around the place, so he made a worm catcher for Grandpa. It consisted of a metal rod about a foot long with a piece of lamp cord attached to one end for electrical power. This was housed in a four inch long wooden handle about an inch in diameter with a hole at the end for the cord to exit. Just plug it in with an extension cord and you're in business.

This little gadget didn't actually catch worms, but it figuratively shocked their socks off. When the metal probe was shoved into the ground and the cord was plugged in, an electrical current would flow from the rod and agitate the worms so much they would get to the surface as fast as possible. We just picked them up, and then into the coffee can they would go. If, however, one forgot to unplug said device before collecting the worms, you too would be dancing a jig trying to escape the current vibrating the bottom of your feet. This happened to me more than once, but don't tell anybody.

If the fishing day fell on a Saturday, I would grab the bait and walk with Gramps to the pond. Grandpa kept a metal chair under a huge cottonwood tree, but I just usually sat on the bank. The cats would always tag along because they received a little perch snack. When we had enough for supper, Grandpa would catch two or three more and toss them to his little feline buddies. They would climb all over each other trying to get their teeth into a flopping fish in the grass. When our little caravan headed for the house I always thought, "I can't wait till next Saturday, so we can do this again."

After we cleaned the fish in the back yard, the cats also got the heads, fins and guts. The cleaned pieces would then go into Grandma who rolled them in flour and cornmeal and fried them in a cast iron skillet half full of hot Crisco. She also made hush puppies from her mama's recipe. They were about the size of a golf ball, salty, dark brown and crunchy. I wish I had that recipe, but at six years old the recipe wasn't important, just the food. Besides that, the thought of my grandparents dying someday never entered my mind. When they did pass away, Grandma first and then Grandpa shortly thereafter, the words of comfort I heard about them being in a better place didn't actually provide much comfort. All I could think was, "Yeah, that's fine, but what about me!"

How did I get off on all that? As I mentioned previously, Grandpa had two dogs, George and George. George, the hound dog, was the one that attacked my Uncle J.B. on Christmas Eve. He was a large dog who usually just slept in the shade on the porch, not bothering anyone—very unexcitable. But, Santa Claus walking up the driveway with a bag to his porch, at night—ain't gonna happen. But that's another chapter.

George number two was a lab mix of some sort who was more sociable. He was snow white except for a quarter sized black dot on his back next to his tail and a little black trim around the edges of his ears. He weighed about sixty pounds and always wore a smile. He hung out with George number one most of the time, but when I would come over for a visit he wanted my attention, so we would have long conversations about the things that mattered most. Like, please scratch my ears and let's go chase the cats. I don't remember how Grandpa acquired the dog, but he was part of the family.

After a while he began to follow me home and I would take him back time and time again until one day Grandpa spoke up and said, "You want that dog?" My eyes got as big as saucers and I said, "I sure do." He said, "Well, you can just keep him." I was the happiest kid in the world. The dog was listening to us and knew what was going on as I gave him a big hug. I told him on the way home that he needed a new name. We both agreed on "Jack." Jack was my best friend and was by my side every day until he died of old age.

We would sit together under a big shade tree in the back yard and make plans. Jack would give me a long stare and ask me, "What do you want to do next?" I would give some thought to the question and run some options by him. When I suggested something he liked, he would wag his tail to let me know that was the best idea and off we would go. Someone had trained Jack in voice commands, and he knew them all. I never had to get him worked up and excited or employ other human tactics to get him to do something. All I had to do was calmly speak the word, and he would gladly obey.

My dad and mom liked to fish, and about once a week we would pack a lunch and load up Dad's 1948 Dodge. It had running boards, suicide doors and rode like a dream. Dad, being a mechanic, kept it tuned up and looking good.

Dad was constantly discovering a new secret fishing hole. He liked secluded farm ponds the best, and how he found these places I'll never know. One Saturday morning just as the sun was coming up, I found myself on the bank of an overgrown, snake infested creek that ran through some guy's land who was a friend of my Dads. Big fish were in there all right, but actually getting to the water was the problem. Hey, we're outside fishing, it's not cold or raining so why complain?

Jack hadn't been a member of the family for very long, and Dad let me bring him along. He was exploring in the brush by the water's edge about thirty feet from me, when all of a sudden, I heard something hit the water with a crash followed by frantic splashing noises. Dad and I ran down there to check out the commotion. Somehow, Jack had slipped and fell into the water. Much to our surprise, we found out that he couldn't swim. Dad jumped in and drug him out. We were all relieved and wet, so we decided to pack up and get out of there. After everyone was dried off, we went to a pond east of Morris with gently sloping banks and stocked with largemouth bass. Mom hung one so big that he snapped her pole. She grabbed the line and pulled him in while walking backwards.

We had a parakeet that stayed in a bird cage by the window most of the time. He would chirp and sing as the sun came up and filled his little wire house with light. His name was "Pete" and he was the only animal that Mom would allow in the house. Consequently, Jack stayed outside but didn't seem to mind as long as he could go inside Dad's shop to get out of the weather. We didn't buy dog food. Jack ate what we ate. We didn't take him to the Vet because he was never sick.

My bedtime was eight p.m., and I went to sleep pretty fast. So by four thirty in the morning, I was all rested up and ready for action. Excited about another new day, I would put my clothes on, grab my BB gun and exit the back door to meet Jack and his wagging tail. After a brief conversation, we would take off down the gravel road before anyone else was awake. The black sky was filled with big, bright, shining diamonds, and the damp grass shimmered in the starlight. An owl sat on the telephone pole and gave us a friendly "hoot" as we passed beneath his wooden perch. He was a regular and sat up there every night. Coyotes would howl in the distance as they made their way back to their dens after the night's hunt for mice and rabbits. The air was cool and smelled crisp and clean. Well, except of course for the times the odor of some irritated skunk would drift our way. Wait! What was that rustling sound in the ditch? I didn't have a flashlight to see it, but Jack probably knew what it was all along.

We would spend an hour or so walking the country roads, shooting at pop bottle caps or beer cans in the ditch just for practice. Talking to each other quietly, sometimes Jack would relay to me one of his one liners and we would both laugh.

Jack passed away quietly one cold night in February, but he has never left my heart. He's in heaven now. I'll see you again, Jacky. We'll run and play again.

Country Girl

Grandma set aside one day a week for baking, usually desserts, although she made her own loaves of bread and rolls, also. If she had leftover fruit, she would roll out her dough in a small circle and spread out the apples, plums or berries on top, add a little sugar and then fold the dough over and pinch the edges together. Then she would place them into a cast iron skillet half full of hot grease. In about five minutes, they were done and ready to come out of the skillet to cool down on a towel covered metal pan. You can't hardly beat a golden-brown fried pie.

She usually did all of this on Saturday, so I could follow that wonderful aroma as I walked to her house to watch her bake and listen to stories about her childhood. She grew up between Warner and Webber Falls, Oklahoma as Alma Elizabeth Hensley and, like most country girls; she fed the cows, pigs and chickens every morning before getting cleaned up and eating breakfast. Then it was off to school, singing a song as she walked along.

On rare occasions, in the winter months, her dad would let her ride his horse, Old Buck, to school, if he wasn't using him for work on the farm. She could get two of her friends up on the horse's back with her and off they would go. She used the wooden fence for a ladder, no need for a saddle or blanket, just the reins.

Grandma said she loved the smell of that horse on a cold, winter morning and liked to watch his breath shoot two feet out from his nostrils as he walked down the dirt road toward the schoolhouse. When school was over for the day, if there wasn't a ball game or other after school activities, she would treat Old Buck to an apple or carrot and then up on his back for the ride home.

After she brushed the horse down and put him in the barn, it was time to take care of the rest of the animals, bring the firewood in, help her mom with supper and then wash the dishes. She then had time to do her homework and sew. After reading her Bible, it was off to bed. Tomorrow would be a new day and maybe she would get to ride Old Buck again.

Chicken Yard Drama

My grandpa, John Buster Wadley, was a farmer and horse trainer. If he ever lost a game of checkers or dominoes, I don't know about it. My Uncle Carl had a custom game table made for him so he could beat the socks off everybody in style. It had rows of little holes drilled at each player's station that would accommodate golf tees for keeping score. Each hole was five points. Grandpa could not only anticipate your next move, but all your moves! I still don't know how he did it. He totally dominated the game from the first play to the last (his of course).

The South side of his property line was adjacent to our property. If I went to my grandparent's house, I had to walk down the road or take a shortcut through Grandpa's pride and joy: the very large chicken yard, home to about 200 chickens! I never did wear any kind of shoes unless there was snow on the ground, so navigating my way through the minefield of chicken poop was challenging in itself without having to worry about an attack from the rear, literally.

The chicken house was pretty close to the fence. It was made of wood with a dirt floor and had three doors. The door on the right was where the various supplies, buckets, scoops and feed were stored in big steel barrels with metal lids. You wanted metal barrels so the rats couldn't chew through them to get to the grain. The door on the left led to the nesting area. Little dark wooden cubicles stuffed with soft beds of hay, cut from nearby fields lined the walls. Chickens prefer a warm, dark quiet area to lay their eggs. Door number three was on the opposite side of the house and opened into the roosting room. Slats of boards were lined up about three inches apart and four feet from the ground. When the sun goes down, chickens go to bed. They're always anxious to rise in the morning and get to their feed. Their day begins by scratching the ground, rolling in a hole of soft dirt, running from the rooster and laying an egg, in their spare time.

Just west of the henhouse was the storage building that housed Grandpa's multitude of tools. The big work bench had a huge vise mounted on the top along with wooden boxes filled with bolts, nuts, nails and the like. Shelving was attached to the walls and filled with all manner of pulleys, ropes and complicated looking equipment.

This place was like a museum to me. I didn't know what most of this stuff was, and still don't know. If I asked Grandpa about some piece of equipment, he would give me an explanation on how to use it, but I usually couldn't understand what he was talking about, and he was only going to say it once.

It didn't take me long to figure out how to use the vice though. We had hickory and black walnut trees. Both produced nuts that were very tasty but extremely hard to crack. Hitting them with a hammer would work but often smashed them too much. The old vice, however, would apply a little pressure at a time and crack the nuts open just right. Grandma would use the nuts to make tasty treats.

North of the tool shed were three, eight foot square pens, six feet high and totally enclosed with chicken wire. Grandpa and my Dad raised pheasants, also; and kept them in these pens so they couldn't escape. The chicken wire also kept the raccoons, skunks and coyotes out. Those pheasants were mighty fine table fare. I caught a rabbit one time and put him in there, but Dad made me take him out.

A few feet North of the pens was the garden spot. My uncles would haul loads of peanut hulls with their dump trucks to the garden to help break up the soil. Grandpa added chicken poop and horse manure for fertilizer and mixed it all in with a hand plow and shovel. There's nothing better than fresh onions, tomatoes, beans and peas right out of your own garden.

East of the garden was the brooder house used for incubating fertile eggs and keeping baby chicks warm. The brooder house was made of red bricks and was wired for electricity to operate the heat lamps and overhead lights. One hot summer day, I noticed a nasty yellow jacket nest under an eve on the outside of the house. I had gone in and out of there for several days looking at the baby chicks and never noticed it before. I told Grandpa about it and he instructed me to grab the hoe and knock 'em down. I was afraid to do it and told him that plan sounded dangerous. He said I should go ahead, and when I knocked the nest down to just stand "real still" and they would fly away and not bother me. That seemed easy enough. Grandpa's don't lie, right? I proceeded to do as instructed and received five wasp stings on my head before I tore out of there screaming with pain. He lied.

There were gates on the North and South boundaries of the chicken yard. I used these if I took the short cut instead of the road. The task of walking from one gate to another would seem simple enough, but danger lurked in the shadows.

I know this is a revelation to a great number of city folks, but chickens will lay eggs on their own. However, you can't have baby chicks

15

without fertile eggs. You can't have fertile eggs without; you guessed it, a rooster.

Roosters have attitudes. Roosters are bossy. Roosters have over-protection complexes and anger issues. They are armed and dangerous. They have two to three inch spurs on their legs and can use them skillfully. They are territorial. They worry about the hens running away. I don't know why. They're fenced in. Even though he doesn't have to buy them chocolate or take them out to dinner, you would think he just spent his last dime trying to make the girls like him. Hey, where's the competition? He's the only man in the yard.

I had to contend with one of these egomaniacs every time I crossed "the yard." His name was George. Why George you might inquire. Grandpa called everybody George, including me. Names were obviously of little importance to him. The kids were George. The Grandkids were all George. I don't know, maybe he just liked the name.

Anyway, this particular George was tall for a rooster. Tall roosters can jump quite a distance up on one's leg. He was multicolored with golden feathers around his neck, decked out with splashes of black, white and red trim. He had about 500 horsepower with overdrive and for some reason, hated my guts. The feeling was mutual.

After the first unprovoked ambush to the back of my knees from Mr. "G," I was inclined to cut a limb from an elm tree in our back yard. It was about three quarters of an inch in diameter and three feet long. I would call it "Tomahawk." After watching cowboys and indians on television, I learned that the really good gunfighters would carve a little notch in the grip of their revolver each time they shot someone. I decided that this would be an excellent method of tracking the number of times I would manage to land a blow to Mr. "G." This would prove to be more difficult than one might think.

I kept Tomahawk by the gate on my side of the chicken yard fence. I carried the stick from one gate to the other for protection and believe me old George would notice if I forgot it. I had envisioned a long row of notches going the length of Tomahawk, but it never happened. I nailed him three or four times, but that was about it. He was just too slick for me. Hiding behind the chickens to get within striking range, he made sure I was looking straight ahead and then here he would come from my rear, to my rear....end! Traveling at close to 100 mph, he would leap into the air, legs extended, spurs stiff and hit me like a freight train. If I was too slow getting out of there, he would do it again.

By the time I got to Grandma's back door, blood would be running down the back of my legs. Grandpa would start laughing and tease me about letting a little chicken whip my butt. Grandma was much more caring and brought the mercurochrome from the bathroom cabinet and patched up my wounds. I needed sympathy...and a cookie. George died quite suddenly one day from lead poisoning. We had him for supper.

It's a Jungle Out There

My Grandpa worked with a team of horses named Maude and Ball. Strangely enough, he didn't call them both George. They plowed the ground together and made tough jobs look easy. Grandpa was a pro when it came to farming and animals. He never used a veterinarian or farrier but did everything himself from trimming hooves and nailing on horse shoes to floating their teeth. I watched him cram a big wad of Beechnut chewing tobacco down the horses' throats to worm them. He asked me if I wanted to give it a try, but I respectfully declined.

Grandpa had his own field to plow and plant but also did work for other people. When he had a job scheduled, he would get up before daylight to get everything ready and hopefully finish his work before it got too hot.

I remember watching as he put the big harnesses on and ran the long leather straps down the horses' backs so he could guide them. The one man plow was loaded into the back of the buckboard. Blinders were put on the sides of the horses' eyes to keep them focused straight ahead and off they would go to the next field to plow. If the job wasn't too far away, I got to go with him and watch.

Corn was the main crop both for human consumption and feed for the animals. A big field was between Grandpa's property and ours. The dirt was black and fertile and had a fresh, clean smell to it as Maude and Ball pulled that plow and made row after row. After the ground was tilled, it was time to plant the large, dried out yellow seeds and cover them up. After a few days with a little rain and sunshine, the dead seeds turned into moist living plants and began to sprout as their tiny bright green leaves pushed through the dirt seeking the warmth of the sun. Good job, Grandpa.

After a few weeks, those little sprouts turned into huge green corn stalks, shooting up six feet high. It was like having my own personal jungle, dense and even noisy when the hot southern breeze forced its way through the long wide leaves. Jack and I would spend hours in there. What a playground.

As the temperature became hotter, the ears of corn began to form on the cornstalks and here they came. Every summer huge grasshoppers would invade the vegetable garden and fields of corn. They were a brownish color with bright yellow and black wings and made a loud clicking noise when they flew. Grasshoppers are great for fish bait, but these were especially difficult to catch.

Mom made some curtains with her sewing machine and bought new curtain rods to hang them on. The old curtain rods were round, about 3 feet long and a quarter inch or so in diameter. As I retrieved them from the trash can, I'm thinking, "Perfect for a blow gun." I shoved a sewing needle in the end of a wooden match and wrapped the ends of the match with masking tape to increase the diameter and made darts for my curtain rod. It was a perfect weapon to use on those pesky grasshoppers. I practiced a few times shooting at a circle on a cardboard box. The accuracy was perfect, so I was off to the corn field.

My first shot was about six feet away and I hit the mark all right, but instead of falling over, the grasshopper just flew off with my dart. I followed in close pursuit and saw him land about 30 feet away. The weight of the dart caused him to go down and made him easy to catch. I removed the dart and he seemed to be just fine. Into the coffee can he went, and I was off to get another one. I had the same experience with just about every grasshopper but always managed to locate them when they landed, and got my dart back.

Dad made a wooden framed cage for me and covered it with quarter inch hardware cloth. It had a hinged door on one end and was perfect for holding those giant grasshoppers. I stuffed some Bermuda grass inside for food and carried it with me on my future hunting expeditions. We caught some nice sized bass and catfish with those grasshoppers, and Mom knew just how to fry um up for supper.

Dad

Not long after my parents were married, James Thomas Wadley was drafted by the army and shipped overseas to fight the Japanese who were determined to take control of the Philippines. The Japanese Air Force had destroyed our naval fleet of battleships at Pearl Harbor and severely crippled our military. It was time for the United States to kick some butt, and my dad was a part of our victory.

When he finally came home from World War II, Dad was pretty shot up. He was actually shot five times but made it through alive with the wounds and scars as a reminder that freedom isn't free. His right arm was now smaller than his left and had a 9 inch long skin graft scar. There was another long scar across his chest from enemy gunfire, and on a sunny day if he had his shirt off, you could see the lead bullet fragments that remained in both of his shoulders. He said the doctors were too busy with other wounded men to remove the smaller pieces. Also, one of his fingers was shot off. He wouldn't talk about the war, and when I asked him about his missing finger, he would only hold his hand up and tell me that he was picking his nose and a booger bit it.

Dad could fix just about anything. I bought my first car from a neighbor. It was a 1950 Chevy Deluxe Fastback with a three speed standard transmission and a 235 cubic inch six cylinder power plant. The motor had a bad piston rod and made a knocking noise. It would still run but was pretty loud. I was mowing lawns at the time and had over two hundred dollars saved up. That was a lot of mowing at roughly $1.50 a yard. I bought the car for $35.00 and had plenty left over to fix the motor.

Dad said he would make all of the repairs but I had to buy the parts. He said that $40.00 would fix it, but if I wanted to "soup it up," it would cost me $85.00. I spent the $85.00. After pulling the engine completely out, he took it to his shop to make the repairs. When the job was complete, he had the motor running while it was still sitting on blocks out of the car!

When all of the mechanical work was completed, I installed a new interior and a new set of tires. Nice ride. After owning the car for a few years, I sold it to a man in Texas and bought a 1965 Chevy with their new hot rod motor, a 396 Turbo Jet. It was a really nice car, but I wish I had kept the old fastback.

Dad was employed at the Phillips 66 refinery for a few years, and after the refinery closed. He bought three service stations with mechanic bays and operated an insurance business on the side. Somehow he always had time to take us fishing. The results of the battlefield claimed his life when he was only 48.

My brother, Jim, passed away recently and left me some of Dad's military items that I didn't know he had. He had a cedar chest that Dad made when he was 16 and a lot of his military stuff was in there. There were several uniforms, medals and various items he had purchased overseas, as well as a 1940's Rolex he had won in a poker game. In a box at the bottom were some papers, one of which was an award for the bronze star from the U.S. Army. I never knew he received it. He never mentioned it. My Dad, a war hero, and I had no idea.

Arthur and Bess

One of Grandpa's buddies, whom he loved to play checkers and dominos with, was his brother and best friend, Arthur Wadley. They would walk or ride a horse to visit with each other about once a week. Arthur was a quiet man like Grandpa so the conversational greetings were short and sweet and usually ended with, "Come on in." What that meant was, "pull up a chair and let's play checkers." After a few fast-paced games and less than a dozen words spoken, one of them would blurt out, "that's it for me" and the games would end. The two brothers always kept their pocket knives sharp, and I guess a few games of checkers per week kept their minds sharp as well.

Arthur's wife was an American Indian woman named Bess. A more likeable soul you would never meet. Always laughing and carrying on, Aunt Bess was a joy to be around. Never depressed or sad about anything, she was always an encouragement to everyone she came in contact with.

The Wadley family members always had big vegetable gardens, and it was fun to see how each one planted their favorite foods. I would ride my bicycle over to see how Aunt Bess was coming along with her canning. She loved to show off what she had put up in her root cellar in the backyard, so off we would go, flashlight in hand down to the dungeon. The cellar door was above ground level and steps descended down into the coolness of the pitch black underground room. She had to use a flashlight to see, and as Aunt Bess scanned the old wooden shelves, she would show me the Mason jars filled with fruits and vegetables grown in her backyard. Impressive? Yes, very. Scary? Yes, very. The air was thick and the smell of the earth would fill my nostrils as I kept a lookout for copperheads, black widow spiders and anything else that could bite or sting. I was always excited to visit the cellar and greatly relieved to get out of there.

Everyone canned in my family and during those cold winter months we always had plenty of beans, potatoes, beets, tomatoes and the like right from the jar. My wife, Christie, still cans what we grow at our house, and she's become quite the expert at it. She puts a label on each jar and the date, also. This tells us what we've got and when it was canned. It's a huge, time consuming process with all of the food preparation, measuring and timing. The pressure canner must be watched continuously and turned off at just the right time. When the task is complete and you gaze at all of the brightly colored jars, full of all that good stuff lined up in neat little rows, you can say, "job well done," followed closely by, "I need a nap." I'm just glad that she does it all and not me.

Loft Apartment

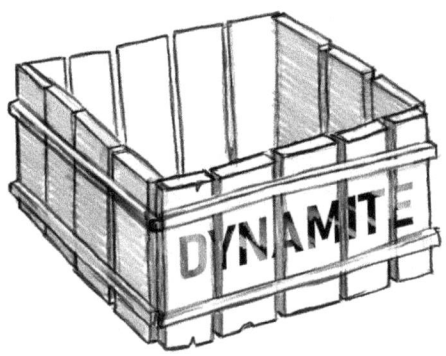

Grandpa's horses stayed in the barnyard when they weren't working. They were fed from feed troughs located inside their stalls in a huge barn made of cedar planks. J.B., Carl and James, Grandpa's sons, built the barn and laid it out just right. There were two large, sliding doors, one on each end, North and South. The west side was composed of four horse stalls with a vertical row of shelves in each one. On the east side was the tack room, storage for the grain and a big bin for the fresh corn that was grown just across the fence.

One day, I was in the tack room trying to figure out how all of this equipment would fit on a horse and noticed a brown wooden box with a hinged lid. Labeled with black paint on the side was the word "dynamite." I carefully raised the lid and peeked in. There they were. I counted seven sticks of the powerful explosive, and I liked anything that went "boom." Hey, this would be better than a whole box of M80's. Grandpa was close by in the chicken pen, so I yelled out and asked him if we could light a stick and blow something up. He stopped what he

27

was doing and walked over to the barn. After squirting out a stream of Beechnut chewing tobacco, he looked at me and calmly said, "George, leave that box alone." That's all it took. I got the message. I never touched it again.

Inside the barn, not too far from the feed bin, was a wooden ladder that went ten feet straight up to my most favorite place in the world, the hay loft. The sweet smell of freshly cut Bermuda grass would fill the entire barn. Located at the South end of the loft was a 4X4 foot opening used for loading hay bales into the loft. I would sit up there on a bale of hay and do my homework. I could see for miles. It was so peaceful and quiet and overlooked the corn field. I never wanted to come down.

The Hideout

Just on the West side of old Highway 75 was a wooded area thick with vines and heavy vegetation. You couldn't actually walk through it, but Jack and I forged a path down a steep slope which went down about 12 feet or so as the sunlight quickly faded. I had to slide down on my rear because of the overgrowth. It's hard to believe now that I actually went down there, but when I was a kid, I never thought about the danger involved. Plus, I had my best buddy with me who feared nothing.

I don't know who the property belonged to and I'm sure my Mama didn't know about it. If she had seen this place, that would have been the end of my hideout.

So you might wonder what the big attraction was. Well, located at the bottom of the hill was an old rusty car with no door on the passenger side. So, I just slid into the floorboard and hopped over to the driver's side. The thing looked like something Bonnie and Clyde drove. The stick shift and steering wheel were still intact so I pretended I was barreling down some old dusty road at a high rate of speed. I made my own engine and gear grinding noises which was enough to shoo away the rats and copperheads. I guess it worked because I never saw one. But looking back, I know now that there had to have been an angel riding shotgun.

Did someone have a wreck and roll the car down the hill? Who knows? I chose to believe it was bank robbers who were shot by the cops and crashed it after a gun blazing chase.

When we finished our "driving" adventure, Jack and I would crawl out of the old clunker and back up the hill. After brushing the dirt off my pants and picking the thorns out of my arms, we headed back home. Or wait; maybe stop by to see what Grandpa was doing. He usually had a little something for me to do.

Mud Bugs

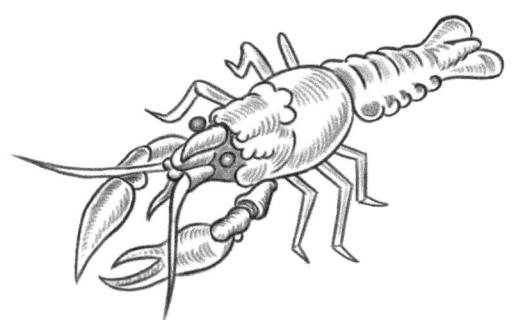

After a good summer rain the ditches filled up with water and forced the crawdads out of their little muddy houses. Jack and I would grab a bucket and head out to see how many we could catch. They were pretty easy to see if the water was clear but always put up a fight. Their only weapon is their pincers, and if they can't escape by swimming backwards, they will stand their ground, pincers waving back and forth above their head ready to latch onto your fingers. I would move quickly, grab them by the back and put them in my bucket. Sometimes I would let the smaller ones pinch me; just to see how it felt. The four-inchers and larger, however, could draw blood and make you holler, "Hidey ho!"

Mr. and Mrs. Graham lived a short distance from us. They didn't have a regular fish pond, but they did have a fantastic crawdad hole. It was a ratty looking, horse shoe shaped body of water about 30 feet across and 2 feet deep. It never went dry, so an underground spring must have supplied water to it. Located in a thickly wooded section of their property, nobody even knew it was there. Mr. Graham showed me where it was and gave me permission to fish for crawdads anytime I wanted. The water always appeared to be dark because of the shade from the willow trees I guess, and I could never really see below the surface.

How does one catch these little critters if you can't even see them, you might ask. The answer: America's favorite health food, bacon. Yep, bacon on a string. It kinda has a nice ring to it, doesn't it?

My Dad instructed me to cut a straight, stiff tree limb and cut off the excess sprouts. About a half inch in diameter and four feet long would be about right. Next, I tied a strand of nylon cord to the end of it. Fishing line is too thin and will tear through the meat. Next, I asked my Mom for a strip of bacon, and I was all set for some cheap entertainment. I cut off a two inch piece of the bait and tied it in the middle with the end of my cord. I'm excited.

I made a bucket for my catch from a blue and yellow, "Miss Tuckers" lard pail. I used an ice pick and poked two holes opposite each other close to the top and attached a piece of bailing wire for a handle. My gear selection was now complete. Jack knew what I was up to when I grabbed that bucket. At least that's what he told me, but I think he just smelled the bacon. Not one to beg, he would just sit real pretty and stare, hoping for a little treat.

With my best friend at my side, I grabbed my BB gun, bucket and bait. We're off to the crawdad hole. We walked down the hot gravel road a short distance and then through a barbed wire fence crossing a cow pasture, always with a sharp eye out for the big red bull. He never really bothered me except for one time when he lowered his head in my direction and pawed the ground a couple of times throwing dust into the air. I don't know if this was an act of aggression or he was just saying "howdy," but I kept my distance after that little incident. After crossing the fence on the other side of the pasture, we reached our destination.

Jack made himself comfortable in the tall grass as he watched all around for outlaws who might try to sneak up on us. I lowered my line into the water and waited for the scent of the bacon to wake everybody up down there. When crawdads attack the bait with their pincers, it feels like a perch hitting a worm with light tackle. After a minute or two, I felt a sharp tug and then another and another. I slowly pulled my line out of the water and over to the lard bucket to shake off the hungry little critters. Sometimes I just caught one at a time, but other times, there were three or four. They landed in the bottom of the bucket with a clang. Jack would get up and come over to look in the bucket and wag his tail with excitement. The first time we did this, he jerked his head out of the bucket with an agitated mud bug attached firmly to his nose. He let out a painful yelp and knocked it off with his paw. Being the fast learner that he was, he kept a safe distance after that. When we had caught enough bait to go fishing at Pollard's pond, it was back to the house to get the fishing pole and tackle box, after Jack ate the bacon that we didn't use, of course. Good boy!

Trapped Like a Rat

Attending school was never my cup of tea. It became a little easier as I grew older, but the whole concept of sitting in a little room at a little desk unarmed, without my dog, all day long made no sense to me. I felt like I was in a trap. My birthday was in October so I was always the youngest one in my class, which made things more difficult. They should have waited another year before making me go, but I had absolutely no say in the matter. So there I was, day after day with a bunch of little kids studying out of little books. What a way to grow up. *Eye shud be wabbit huntin somwhere insted of lernin how to spel.*

Life wasn't all bad, though. I had a Big Chief writing tablet with the chief's picture on the front cover. It had big wide lines on the pages on which I wrote with my big fat pencil these words, "I do not want to be here." Actually, I always wanted to be an Indian chief, and I guess that's why I liked the tablet. My dad even bought me a set of Indian clothes with feathers and all. It was my favorite outfit. That is of course until the Lone Ranger outfit hit the market, which included a cool black mask. My mother drove me to school the first couple of weeks and then walked with me a time or two to show me the shortcuts. After that, Jack would tell me goodbye from the front porch and watch as I walked away with my Big Chief tablet and a fried egg sandwich.

We lived in the country so the shortest route was by climbing through two barbed wire fences and crossing a huge cow pasture with a pond. After that, I could walk down a paved road until I reach a street with a sidewalk on each side. I had the option of using either the sidewalk or the street, if no cars were coming. From there, it was a straight shot to Wilson Elementary School.

There were two first grade teachers at the school, and I was fortunate to have Mrs. Baldwin. She was very kind and did her best to help me adjust to the classroom setting. I walked by her house every day. She had an aluminum storm door with a big "B" in the middle of it which I thought was cool. I think that door is still on the house. If she happened to see me walking or riding my bike, sometimes she would invite me in for a cookie or two. Her house had that smell of old wood and old books lined the shelves. It was always fun to talk to her and we remained buddies for quite a few years.

Each school day began with music. Our *National Anthem* was played and broadcast via a microphone set next to the speaker of a record player. If you were a good student, you may be selected to place the old scratched up 45 rpm record on the turntable which was centrally located in the auditorium/gymnasium/lunchroom. A bell would ring and each class would stand and face the large American flag that was proudly displayed in the corner of the room as the "hiss" of static signaled the beginning of the song. After that, we covered our hearts with our right hand and loudly proclaimed the *Pledge of Allegiance*. With our engines all warmed up, we were ready for the day.

One day after school, I was walking home and Gloria, who was in my class, was walking with me. She only lived a few blocks away. We were talking about important stuff like dogs and candy. I mentioned that I was going fishing with my dad the next Saturday and I was excited about it. That's when Gloria told me that her dad lived in another state and she and her mom lived here. When I asked why her dad didn't live with them, she said it was because they were divorced. We had reached her house by this time, and I walked on home pondering about what she had just said. I had no idea what she was talking about and never had I heard the word "divorce" before. When I got home, the first thing I did was ask Mom if she knew what divorce meant and when she told me, I just couldn't believe it. I thought when people married, they stayed together no matter what, just like Grandma and Grandpa.

The Mormon Board

Mr. and Mrs. Pollard lived across the road from my grandparents. Dortha, their daughter, lived with them. They had two sons, Glenn and Bobby. Glenn was more of a business man and I don't remember what Bobby did for a living, but I was more acquainted with him. He was a great guy. Mr. Pollard was in the oil drilling business and had a parcel of land next to the house filled with pipe, sucker rods, trucks and drilling equipment. I had permission to hunt cottontails on the property, which I did regularly. The rabbits loved those big eight inch pipes. They would hide in there and were protected from coyotes and bobcats. I would chase them from one pipe to the next trying to get a shot. Every once in a while, I would get a couple for supper, but most of the time, they were just too fast for me. If you've never had fried rabbit, you're missing a great treat. We don't eat that much rabbit here in the United States, but in Europe they raise huge rabbits just to eat, like we raise chickens and turkeys.

My Dad brought home six white rabbits one time. Someone he worked with had given them to him. He gave them to me, a buck and five does. They were so cute, friendly and tame, and became my pets. I gave them all names and would sit in the backyard and play with them while they chewed on grass and clover. Pretty soon we were building rabbit pens like crazy to keep up with the growing bunny family. Forget that naming business, they all looked exactly alike. I had little white rabbits everywhere and a string of houses that stretched all the way across the backyard.

All of my lawn mowing money was spent on rabbit pellets and things were getting way out of hand. My Mom put her foot down one day and told me that this operation had to come to an end. I reluctantly sold my 126 furry friends to a nice old man for a dollar each.

Walking sadly away from the sale of my little white buddies, I felt that huge wad of money in my pocket as my mind contemplated my next investment: quail, baby calves or maybe a pony... hum.

Mr. Pollard wanted to put a few cows in his pasture to help keep the grass down and supply the family with fresh meat. There was just one problem. He had no water supply. One day Grandpa and I were in the front yard cleaning out the flower beds, when Mr. Pollard walked over to chat. "John," he said. "Can you dig a pond for me with your horses?" Grandpa responded with the equivalent of "no problem" and asked him how big he wanted it. Did you know it was possible to dig a pond with a team of horses? I didn't either. A bulldozer could dig it maybe, but not an old man and a couple of horses.

As the three of us walked down to the East end of the pasture to scope out the situation, I remember thinking that Gramps was in over his head on this one. I watched as they drove a few pieces of sucker rods into the ground to mark the boundaries and shook hands. I don't know how much money they agreed on, if any. Grandpa liked to fish and a new pond would be very convenient. This may have been a mutually beneficial situation; I don't know and never really thought about it at the time.

About a week later, I walked home from school and saw Mom in the front yard. She told me Grandpa had started on the pond. I was ready to see this. I dropped my books off on the front porch and took off running to the job site. Jack was by my side and inquired as to why the big rush. I tried to explain to him what was going on but he didn't understand. For that matter, I didn't exactly know what I was talking about either. I was just excited.

We both arrived out of breath and began watching Grandpa, Maude and Ball at work. Grandpa was in high gear moving dirt. The big strong horses had their plowing harnesses on, but instead of a plow they were pulling a large, heavy metal blade. It was angled so that it would re-move a few inches of soil as it was pulled by the team. Grandpa was standing on top of the big tool to provide the necessary added weight.

He had a leather rein in each hand and would go round and round, removing a little dirt with each pass.

Jack and I sat on the ground and watched Grandpa and his team until it began to get dark. Grandpa disconnected the blade and left it where it was, and then, with a rein in each hand, he walked behind the horses and headed home. I was walking beside him and asked what that blade was. He said it was a "Mormon Board." I don't know what became of that "Mormon Board" but I've never seen another one.

Every day Jack and I would run down to check out the progress, and every day a little more dirt was dug out and piled up on the bank. Finally, one day it was over. The task was complete. The pond was built. It looked really deep to me, but I think it was just about five feet.

Each time we had a good rain the pond would fill up a little more and pretty soon it was at maximum capacity. Grandpa put an overflow on the far North end and the excess water would drain out into a ditch along the side of the road. Grass began to grow over the bank and it was time to start putting fish in there.

After a family fishing trip, we would eat the big fish that we caught but kept the smaller ones alive and put those in the pond. Everything, from catfish to bass and crappie, was dumped in there, but mostly perch. They don't get as big as the other fish, but they are quite the little fighters when hooked. I have great memories of that pond.

Dad at Clayton Lake

Dad in Luzon

Dad, JB and Carl

Dad

Grandpa Wadley with Maude and Ball

Jack and Me

Jim

Me

Mom, Jim and Dad

Mom

Mom

My brother Jim

Uncle Carl

Fine Music, Ultimate Sports and the Gospel Truth

M y Grandparent's sons were good men. They worked hard and had their own businesses. They loved their parents and appreciated them. If their mom or dad needed anything, they would make sure they got it. Consequently, Grandma had the biggest television obtainable. All three channels were in black and white because color television had not been invented yet, but with a little fine tuning, it produced a pretty clear picture.

Grandma had three shows she liked to watch so she would set aside a couple of hours each day for her viewing pleasure. This was late in the afternoon, so sometimes I would join her after school. Grandpa spent most of his time outside but he would come in once in a while and take a little TV break. We would grab a couple of chairs from the kitchen table while Grandma turned on the set. There were no remote controls back then. If you wanted to change the channel you had to get up and turn the knob and adjust the picture for clarity. This was like going to the movies for me, and I could hardly wait for the first show, Hovie Lister and the Southern Gospel Quartet.

A half dozen quartets would perform in each show with usually just a piano for the instrument and maybe a guitar player every once in a while. Occasionally, women would perform, but most of the time it was all men. All four singers dressed exactly the same, usually in dark suits with white shirts and black ties. There was no need to wear different colors on television I guess; it was all black and white anyway. The men had shiny black hair and had it slicked down with about a quart of *Vitallis* hair oil, ultra-cool.

They always had a piano solo and man would they cut loose. The musicians would pound those ivory keys as their hands shot up past their shoulders. It was like the keyboard was spring loaded. You couldn't stop patting your foot during the entire show.

If you've ever heard a professional gospel quartet perform, you know that the harmony is outstanding. No one was out of pitch and those piano players never missed a note. My favorite singer was the bass. He was usually a tall skinny guy with sunken eyes and a protruding Adams apple the size of a goose egg. I would try to sing along, but when he dropped an octave to hit those seemingly impossible low notes, there was no way.

Grandma knew what it meant to be washed in the blood. I could see the tears fill her eyes when the boys would sing "Amazing Grace" and it seemed like God was right there in the room with us. I know now that He really was.

The last song of the show was always upbeat and all of the singers had a short solo. Hovie always wrapped it up with a piano solo, but then, suddenly and sadly, the announcer would say, "See you next time and God Bless." It was over. Silence filled the living room. But wait! What's coming on next?

I don't know what it is with old ladies and wrestlers, but there's definitely a connection there. I don't think Grandma ever actually attended a live wrestling match, but she never missed one on television. Yes, sir, right after the southern gospel music show came Championship Wrestling. I have to admit, it was pretty exciting watching a bunch of 350 pound characters throw each other all over the ring.

My wife's grandmother, Ola, had the same attraction for the large men in tights. She would get all gussied up and drive her car around to pick up her three fat friends once a week and off they would go to the Coliseum in Fort Worth, Texas. I'm sure they had ringside seats.

There were always the good wrestlers and the really evil wrestlers. They were paired against each other and the crowd would boo and cheer as they waited impatiently for the starting bell to ring.

I attended a match with a friend of mine one time, and he wanted the autograph of one of the bad guys. I think his name was Al "the spider" Galento. Big Al had very long arms and legs, thus the nickname, "The Spider." Al, being a bad guy was also very rude and sneaky, so after we got his autograph he kept my friend's ink pen and quickly stuck it inside the waistband of his wrestling trunks. I don't recall the good guy opponent's name, but soon after the match began Al retrieved the ink pen and commenced to rake it across the forehead of his opponent. Blood flew everywhere and the crowd began to roar. One of Al's buddies threw a folding chair into the ring, and Al used it on the top of the guy's head causing him to crash to the mat. It was over. The Spider had won.

Grandma was a devoted fan of the Great Bolo, a good guy who always wore a mask. The men he fought against were constantly trying to rip the mask off, however, no one ever succeeded. There were many fans on both sides of the fence, but the truth be known, the majority loved the bad guys. They received all of the "boos" and "hisses," but that was half the fun of watching.

I worked part time at my Uncle Joe's Phillips 66 gas station when I was a little older. The station was open 24 hours, and I was working the night shift when I was about 15 years old. The gas stations back then were service stations, meaning full service. You didn't pump your own gas. The attendant did that for you. Not only that, but we would also check your oil, air up your tires, clean your car windows, even on the inside if the customer wanted and last but not least, vacuum the floor boards and seats. We wore uniforms and caps and our closest competition was the Texaco station across the street. Our goal was to give better service than anyone else in town, and that's exactly what we did. And what was my pay for all of this service? Thirty-five cents an hour.

One night after I patched the tubes on a stack of flat tires and hosed down the wash bay and the lube bay, I sat down at the front desk and proceeded to get busy on a little homework. Things were pretty slow after midnight, but about 1:00 am the driveway bell rang signaling a customer at the gas pump. As I approached the car, I could see forearms hanging out the windows that were of massive diameter. When I got closer, I recognized the driver. It was Danny Hodge, a big time good guy wrestler. Sitting on the passenger's side was, I can't believe it, "The Spider." I was a little obvious, but I quickly looked in the back seat and there sat Sputnik Monroe, evil guy, and another huge man that I didn't recognize, but due to his build, I had to ask. "Are you the Great Bolo?" I said. He just gave me a big grin. Unbelievable. Here were the biggest "foes" on television, laughing and yucking it up like kids at a birthday party. I was devastated. I felt betrayed. After that night, I could never think of professional wrestlers the same way again. Somehow all of the excitement went out of the whole experience. Alas, the good versus evil part was just showbiz. I never told my grandmother about what I had seen. She would have either passed out on the floor or accused me of lyin'.

After the rasslin was over, we had one more program to watch, Oral Roberts. Oral traveled around and held his meetings in tents, huge tents. He was tall and handsome and his ministry was mainly praying for the sick people. I remember when early in his ministry some drunk man took a shot at him while he was preaching. This attack just helped to make Oral more famous, and the crowds grew larger by the thousands.

When the tent was packed with people, workers would roll up the sides so the crowds could expand past the boundaries of the tent. I've never seen anything like it.

Oral had jet black hair and dressed in black slacks and tie with a white shirt. He would stand and teach, building up the faith of the people, proclaiming the good news of how God wanted everyone to be healed of their infirmities. When he finished teaching, a long line would form and one by one the sick and lame would come to have hands laid on them as Oral commanded them to be healed in Jesus name. People jumped up out of wheelchairs, blind eyes were opened, the deaf could hear, tumors disappeared and miracle after miracle happened as the power of God flowed through that place. By the time the service was over, the wheelchairs and crutches would be piled up several feet high, and the healed people were jumping and running around shouting for joy.

My Grandma made sure that I witnessed these miracles. She wanted me to know what God was really like, and I'll never forget those good times in front of the television. After watching our three programs, we were fired up and ready for a game of checkers. Maybe I can beat Grandpa this time.

Put Me on the Food Channel

I grew up with a family of great cooks. The men were masters of the charcoal grill, and we had great times at family get togethers. I learned from my Dad and Uncle Carl how to grill hamburgers, steaks, fresh vegetables and thick slices of buttered garlic bread. That smoky flavor made everything taste wonderful.

The women baked, made candy, you name it, and they could do it. I would watch intently as they worked away using the same techniques their mothers used. My grandmother made the best biscuits in the world, and I regret not learning exactly how she did it. Grandpa just loved them, so she made them every morning and could probably have done it blindfolded. She would knead the dough out into a cylinder shape, about two inches in diameter, and then pinched it off with her index finger and thumb and place the final product on the baking sheet. They looked like big white Hershey Kisses all lined up in neat rows. Grandpa said they looked like cat heads so he called them "cat head" biscuits. What I didn't pay attention to was the ingredients she put in the dough. I've tried time and again to duplicate her recipe, but to no avail. Maybe it was just all that extra love she put in there.

Dad liked to expand his horizons with the food scene and consequently had a flair for weird stuff like calf brains and pickled pig's feet. On occasion, he would scramble a cast iron skillet full of eggs with calf brains and then tell me after breakfast what I just ate. He would go after those pig's feet like a hungry dog on a T-bone, so I just had to give'em a try. No thanks. Can't handle it. That strong smell of vinegar would open up your sinuses all right, but between that and thinking about what that pig had been walking through all his life turned me off to the pig's feet. Now bacon, well, that's another story.

Dad was, however, the expert at making homemade peppermint ice cream, or "peckermint" as he called it. After emptying several bags of candy onto a clean towel, he would fold the towel over and beat the daylights out of it with a hammer until the little pieces were just the right size. Into a big bowl it would go with several cartons of whipping cream, untold amounts of sugar and a secret ingredient or two. After it was all mixed together, he poured it into the metal canister of the "hand cranked" ice cream mixer. After being lowered into a wooden bucket, the crank mechanism was latched to the top. Ice and rock salt were added between the canister and bucket as needed. Towels were placed on the top so my butt would stay relatively dry, and there I sat while Dad turned the crank. It seemed like forever, but eventually, the crank handle would become difficult to turn which meant the cream was firm and ready to eat. Actually, it was ready in about thirty minutes, but it seemed like hours to a hungry kid. I forgot all about my frozen rear end when it was time to eat the cream.

For Sunday dinner, we usually had chicken. Mom would pick out a fat hen from the flock and proceed to grab it by the head and vigorously sling it around in a circle until the head came off. The headless hen would flop around wildly slinging blood all over the back yard as Jack and I watched this horrifying ordeal and thinking that there must be a nicer way to kill a chicken. This process lasted way too long for me, and I was officially not hungry anymore.

When the action stopped, the dog and I checked ourselves over for spots of blood and watched as Mom proceeded to dunk the dead chicken into a tub of boiling water to loosen up the feathers for easier plucking. After removing the feathers, the carcass was brought into the kitchen to be cleaned up, battered up and rolled up in Martha White flour. When the skillet full of Crisco was hot, the pieces were crammed in to fry until golden brown and crunchy. The pieces were then removed and allowed to drain and dry. All of those little crunchy pieces of flour and chicken left in the pan were used to make gravy. Mom browned some flour in the skillet and then added milk and seasoning while stirring slowly as the mixture thickened to a perfect consistency. Suddenly, my appetite returned. You just can't beat chicken gravy on top of home grown mashed potatoes. A lot of preparation, but it was well worth the effort. Thanks Mom, for all of those delicious meals.

When I was big enough to find my way around the kitchen, I decided that I would be the breakfast cook for the family. Mom said she didn't mind if I gave it a try, so when Jack and I returned home from our early morning jaunts, he would take a little nap in the yard and I would go inside, wash my hands and get busy in the kitchen. It was still an hour or so before daylight, so I had plenty of time to put it all together.

Good old Folgers coffee was the first order of business. I filled the bottom of the drip coffee maker with water, loaded the top section with ground coffee, put the lid on and set it on the gas burner on low heat. In about 10 minutes, the smell of freshly brewed coffee filled the house. I didn't drink the stuff but enjoyed watching my parents have a cup and tell me that I did it just right. Dad always poured his in a saucer to cool it down a bit and then he just slurped it right out of the saucer. How cool is that?

I checked out the ice box to see what kind of meat I could fry up. It was usually bacon, sausage or baloney. But one time, I discovered some left over catfish in there and used that. Fish for breakfast seemed like a good idea to me but nobody else seemed to appreciate the smell of fried fish at 6 o'clock in the morning, so from then on, I stuck with the basics.

Biscuits from scratch were a challenge, but I gave it my best shot—although canned biscuits were a lot less trouble. Fresh chicken eggs were fried up in the skillet and there you have it, breakfast on the table. Top it all off with homemade butter and blackberry jelly. Now that's a meal. It was time for me to get ready for school while Mom cleaned up and washed the dishes.

Camping Out

Fishing was our thing; so, we spent many Saturdays on the banks of farm ponds or at the lake. We also camped out quite a bit usually at Clayton or Greenleaf Lake. My Aunt Irene kept a "camping box" in her garage! I guess because she had the extra room for it. It took two people to move it around because of its size. It looked kind of like an oversized cedar chest. There was a big open compartment in the bottom where the camping gear was. Sheets, blankets, pillows and the like were stored in there. Right above that was a huge tray that was sectioned off where our eating utensils were. We didn't have plastic; so, real silverware was in these compartments along with food spices, metal cups and plates, dishtowels, clothes pins and anything else one might need for a stay in the great outdoors.

My Dad, his brothers, sisters and in-laws all contributed to the contents of the box. When we got ready to go camping, we would grab the camping box and take off. Sometimes the whole clan would go. There would be four or five carloads of us heading out to jerk the jaws off some bass. If I was fortunate enough to catch a ride with my Uncle Carl, he would put me in charge of opening cold beers and passing them over.

We had a family boat also. My Dad, J.B., Carl and Joe Weller all pitched in and bought it from our cousin Louis Youngblood, who owned Youngblood's Sporting Goods located on East Main Street in Okmulgee, Oklahoma. The boat was a wide bodied 16 foot Lone Star equipped with a 7½ horse power outboard motor. It had bench seats and was very stable in the water, just great for running trot lines.

When we arrived at the lake, the kids would scout around for fire-wood while the men prepared the boat and fishing gear. The ladies unloaded the camping box and set up everything for supper. Hopefully, we would be eating fish in a little while and not baloney sandwiches.

There's nothing quite like the smell of a campfire out by the lake. We would cut marshmallow sticks from the surrounding trees and roast those little sugar balls as soon as we got the fire going. Everyone worked together as a team and we were all set up in no time at all.

The men would usually take the boat out first and bait a trot line with crawdads. The line would be stretched across a narrow body of water about 50 yards or so. About every three feet a short lead line with a hook on the end of it was attached to the main line. All of this would disappear down into the water and the big catfish would grab that crawdad and hook themselves. Leaning over the side of the boat, the guys would pull themselves along checking the hooks for fish and re-baiting if necessary. The line was checked every two or three hours.

We used the old "pump up" Coleman stoves. They were green and had little fold- out shields on both sides to block the wind. The larger stoves had four burners and we used them all. The girls always brought side dishes or vegetables in cans and made cornbread or biscuits to compliment the fish.

Once the fish were skinned and breaded, they were put in the big cast iron skillet that was loaded with hot oil. The smell of that fish along with the campfire is delightful indeed!

We fished from the bank if the boat was occupied and used minnows for bait. Largemouth bass just love minnows, so bass is what we caught, along with a few crappie now and then.

Everyone always had a great time on our camping trips. We only stayed a night or two in most cases and then it was back to work and back to school.

My Dad and I went to Clayton Lake a few years in a row and stayed a week each time. That was a special time for me. We had cots and would just sleep out under the stars.

The lake was small and just perfect for jug fishing. Dad used big treble hooks and beef liver for bait. The big catfish would go after that liver like crazy. We ate catfish all week and would bring home ice chests full for a fish fry.

One night, I was sleeping on my cot. Dad's cot was a few feet away. I woke up about four in the morning to the feeling of something crawling on my legs. I couldn't see what it was, but it was heavy. It scared me so much that I couldn't yell out for help and didn't want to move for fear of provoking the creature. After about a minute that seemed like an hour I felt the intruder jump off my feet and onto the ground. I was greatly relieved, but still too scared to move.

A few minutes later, I heard Dad get up. He was going to get everything ready to check the jugs. I could hear him pumping up the Coleman lantern and when he lit the mantle, I jumped out of that cot and told him what had happened. He took the lantern off the nail in the tree and began to shine the light around the surface of the ground looking for clues. "Here we go," he said as he squatted down and motioned for me to have a look. There they were the clues to solve the case.

It looked to me like hand prints of little long boney fingers. They were all over the place. "It's a coon, and a big one, too," Dad said. He told me that is why we keep all of the food in the truck. Raccoons love to raid campsites and look for free food when they know everyone is sleeping. We left the lantern on at night from then on and had no more "visitors." We went down to the boat to shove off and a big water moccasin came crawling out with his white mouth wide open. Dad killed it with an oar and off we went. Too much drama for one day!

Everything was smooth sailing for the rest of our stay, and we returned home with lots of fish and memories.

Strawberry Fields Forever

I have more relatives than I could ever remember; however, there are a few that are vivid in my memory more than others. My grandmother's brother, Oscar, and his wife Sabra Hensley, lived in Webbers Falls along with several other kin folks who farmed the huge corn fields outside of town. One cousin even flew his own crop-duster airplane over the corn to kill the destructive insects. The Sloans were big time farmers and had the monster machines to get the job done. Matter of fact, they're still in business.

Uncle Oscar built a large, very functional house for their big family. A big, open kitchen complete with a wood burning oven was used during the winter months and also helped to keep the house warm. They used the gas burning oven in the summertime. Water was piped in throughout the house from a spring fed well. It was cold and tasty. The kitchen opened up into a spacious dining room with four doors that could be opened to access the wraparound screened-in porch. This is where we kids would eat, on bench-like wooden tables, custom made by Uncle Oscar.

Once a year, many of the relatives would be invited to a big dinner and entertainment like horseshoes, cards, dominos and checkers. Everyone brought their favorite dish, and Aunt Sabra would fry chicken and bake about a hundred biscuits. The house was surrounded by shade trees and it was fun just to sit out on that porch in the coolness and listen to the leaves rustle in the wind. With the kitchen windows open, the breeze would circulate through the dining room and help to cool down the cooking area.

All of these festivities took place during strawberry season. Along with all of his other talents, Uncle Oscar was a world champion grower of the reddest, juiciest, fattest strawberries you had ever seen. He had rows and rows of raised beds on some acreage just east of the house. They thrived in the fertile Webbers Falls soil. He sold berries by the quart, crate or truckload. Eat a ripe, juicy strawberry and a big grin will soon follow.

After dinner the adults would sit outside under the shade trees, discuss the latest news and tell lies about how big that bass was they caught. The older folks got the chairs to sit on and we kids got the lawn. We would listen intently as the grownups told their stories and laughed about the good times.

When it was about time for everyone to go home, Uncle Oscar would finally make the announcement I had been waiting to hear all day. He would say, "Okay, you kids grab a sack and pick all the strawberries you want and take um home with you." Yeehaw! Off we would go down the rows picking the biggest ones.

After everyone said, "Thanks and Goodbye," we loaded up the car with empty dishes and sacks of strawberries then headed home. I sat in the back seat, of course, to guard the berries.

To Shoot or Not to Shoot

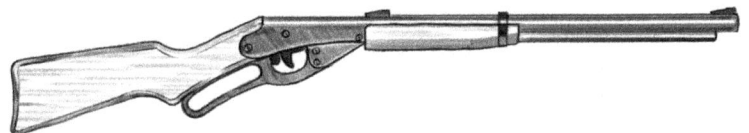

I looked up to my older brother, Jim, and always wanted to participate in whatever he was doing. Jim liked guns, fishing and old cars; so I liked guns, fishing and old cars. He worked at Uncle Joe's gas station and mowed lawns while he was in high school, so I did the same thing. He liked to play the trumpet, so I played the trumpet also. He liked the OSU Cowboys and the Dallas Cowboys; me too. When Jim finished school, he went to work for Texas Instruments in Dallas. Guess what? So did I.

Jim usually got the new stuff when we were growing up, and I usually got his old stuff. "Hand-me-downs," if you will. Shirts, pants, it didn't matter what it was. When he lost interest in his old BB gun that was a good day for me, because it was all mine. It was a Daisy with a wooden stock. By twisting the end of the barrel, a little hole would open and the BB's could be poured in. I don't know how many BB's it would hold, but it was in the hundreds.

I practiced every chance I got with it and became a pretty good shot, although longer distances and windy conditions could be a real challenge. At 350 feet per second, shots out to about 20 yards were pretty easy, and I could dent a Prince Albert can at that distance every time. Shots that were way out there required considerable elevation adjustments.

Rats and mice would frequent Grandpa's chicken house to look for feed on the ground, and they were number one on my hit list. Sneaky and fast they were, and I had to catch um off guard to get a shot. The mice and the smaller rats were pretty easy to kill, but the big rats would just throw their hands up and laugh when I shot them.

Grandma had lots of big trees that housed lots of sparrows that I would occasionally take a shot at. She was okay with that as she watched me out her kitchen window, but if ever I shot at a "songbird" which, in her opinion, was any bird other than a sparrow, Katie bar the door! You would have thought I shot a man in Reno just to watch him die. She would chew me up on one side and down the other. I remember on one occasion, I walked to her house via the chicken yard and she was standing outside by the back door. We were getting ready to go inside when a "songbird" landed in the driveway about 30 yards away. Instinctively, I just took a wild shot from the hip in the general vicinity of the bright red cardinal and watched in terror as it just fell over, dead as a doornail. Grandma lit up like a Christmas tree. She lectured me for 10 minutes as I said, "I was sorry" about a hundred times.

Christmas Eve

M y grandparent's house was the place where the family celebrated the holidays. After a big Thanksgiving feast, one of the family members would write the individual names of all the adults on little pieces of paper and place them in Grandpa's sweat stained felt hat. Each person would then draw out one piece of paper from the hat, and that would be the person they would buy a Christmas gift for. It was a lot easier to buy for one person instead of twenty or so. No one knew who drew their name until the gifts were handed out on Christmas Eve. Grandma and Grandpa weren't included in the name drawing, because they were extra special, and everyone wanted to buy something for them.

We lived just down the road from my grandparents so we always walked down the gravel road for the Christmas Eve Celebration. Our arms full of gifts and tasty dishes that my Mom had prepared as we headed out for Grandma's house. It took us a couple of trips just to get everything delivered, but it was great fun. Everyone was excited, and all of the women were dolled up in their Christmas sweaters and flashy jewelry.

My uncles, J.B., Carl, Joe, George and Charlie and my aunts, Dorothy, Irene, Evelyn, Dixie and Ada Ruth were all there along with my cousins, Steve and Rodney. My cousins were around my age, so we always played together and helped each other get into trouble. But hey, we had fun, well, most of the time.

Evelyn lived in Denver but always returned home and stayed three or four days at Christmas time. She usually brought a few packages of smoked elk with her that was harvested from the good old Colorado Mountains by her two sons, George and Michael. They had a cabin in the high country and always had fresh meat and rainbow trout.

The focal point of Grandma's house was, of course, the kitchen. It wasn't very big and countertop space was quickly covered with platters of baked ham, roasted turkey, homemade rolls, all varieties of vegetable dishes and the like. The aroma was irresistible. The kitchen table was used for a dozen or so pies, cakes, cookies and candy. The "girls" had to skillfully arrange all of that food to produce the best "serve-yourself" experience. Did I mention that the "girls" were just a tad bit competitive? Every dish not only tasted fantastic, but you could observe the hours of preparation that went into each one, from all of those little cloves lined up in perfect rows on the ham to the vivid colors of red and green that popped out at you when the outstanding velvet cake was cut. This was all great for us guys. The men didn't have to do anything except eat and we all did our best to taste a little bit of everything. Hey, you didn't want to hurt anyone's feelings.

The dining room table was a pretty good size but not big enough to accommodate everyone, so we kids got to use the folding card tables that were set up in the living room. The adults used the comfortable dining room chairs and we got the metal folding ones which were fine with me. I was just glad to be there. It was all fun, noisy and exciting.

Finally, someone would say, "Let's open presents." Music to my ears. Everyone got things cleaned up and put away and proceeded to the living room and tried to find a place to sit. We were crammed in there like sardines with the kids on the floor this time.

The girls set up the Christmas tree the week after Thanksgiving. It was always located by the west wall to allow for more of a seating area. The entire West end of the room was stacked high with gifts, not just around the tree, but continuing on to all three walls. It was an awesome sight.

The spirit of competition among the women spilled over from their love of good food to the gift wrapping arena, also. The presents were almost too pretty to unwrap. I said, almost. The colors were bright red, green, yellow, pink, blue, orange and everything in between, and that was just the paper! The bows were always hand made using big, bright ribbons to compliment the paper. Seldom was one ever thrown away. Instead, it was kept and used again on birthdays or wherever a fancy bow was needed.

My Dad on the other hand was a little different story. He preferred to personally wrap the gifts that he gave and they were easily identified. You see, his paper of choice was the daily newspaper. He never had to put his name on anything. If you saw newspaper, you knew who it was from. Much to the disapproval of my wife, I have followed his example. Hey, it's always available and if you're bored you can read your gift while you wait to open it.

Amidst the bright flashes and crackles of Sylvania flashbulbs, more memories began to be recorded on Kodak film. It was a blast to observe the expressions of surprise on the adult's faces when they discovered who had chosen their name out of the hat. My Dad was a mechanic and therefore a tool man. His favorite gift to get was anything used to work on a vehicle. He could rebuild an entire motor. I was watching him installing the bolts on the head of a straight eight engine one time.

I asked how he knew when to quit tightening the bolts. He said, "Right before they break off, you stop."

My grandparents racked up the goods on Christmas Eve. They were given everything they needed and a bunch of stuff that was just for fun. Grandma got stocked up on clothes, bath powder and smelly stuff while Grandpa received enough Beechnut chewing tobacco, Lovera cigars and Old Crow whiskey to last six months. Speaking of Grandpa, I don't know who came up this the idea of a money tree, but he always got one of those too. It kind of reminded you of a scene from the *Godfather*. There he sat in his easy chair with this three foot high tree sitting on the lamp table. Instead of leaves, it had various denominations of money attached to it. I never thought anything about it at the time. It just happened every year at Christmas. Anyway, Gramps loved it. Who wouldn't? I want one. He would also get Christmas cards with cash in them. He would open the card, get the money out and stuff it in his pocket. He then just tossed the card away without reading it. This always bothered me, and I never could figure out why he never cared enough to at least read the card. Instead, he just said, "Thanks." Fast forward about 50 years to my brother and I talking about old times and the subject of Grandpa came up in conversation. We talked about our big Christmas Eve parties, and I asked Jim if he knew why Grandpa never read his cards. He kind of looked at me with a blank stare on his face and explained, "Didn't you know? Grandpa never learned how to read!" All of this time, and I never knew it. Oh well, look at all the junk mail he never had to open.

By the time the last gift was opened everyone was exhausted and ready to go home. We put the house back in order and put all the trash in the burn barrel, packed up our stuff, gave everyone a big hug and said, "Adios."

Walking back to the house with Jack at my side, we could see our breath in the crisp night air. The sky is clear, and the magnificent display of stars sparkles above our heads. Just think. Tomorrow morning is Christmas, and I get to do this all over again.

Kathryn

Ida and Otis lived down the road from us. Good people they were, hard workers and my Mom regarded Ida as her best friend. Kathryn was their daughter. She was a little older than me and considered herself to be smarter and far more mature than me. So, I was a little surprised when she rode up on her bicycle one afternoon just to see what I was up to. Jack and I were sitting on the front porch with a bucket full of crawdads, and I had a couple of them dangling from my fingers. We were easily entertained back then. "What in the world are you doing? Doesn't that hurt?" She proclaimed. "Not bad," I responded. "Would you like to play with one?" I said as I lifted a smaller one from the bucket. "No, I certainly would not." She said as she backed away. That was pretty much the jest of the conversation. I guess my live action figures were a bit extreme for a girl. She said, "see you later" and took off on her bike to visit my Grandma who just happened to be baking oatmeal raisin cookies that day. You got homemade cookies, you got friends.

Jack and I looked at each other and I said, "I don't know why any-one wouldn't want to hold a crawdad." He said that she was just too girly to have any fun with us boys and would probably be happier if she were picking flowers or something. I smiled and Jack got this big grin on his face as I pulled a little larger crawdad from the bucket.

Ida loved to bake and made fresh bread 3 to 4 times a week, and it was melt in your mouth delicious. About a week after our previous visit, Kathryn was knocking on our front door with two loaves of bread. Oh, happy day. My mother had just canned a few jars of blackberry jelly and gave Kathryn a jar to take back home. Both of the women got a big kick out of giving away a portion of the food items they had created, and I got a kick out of eating them.

After chatting with my Mom for a few minutes about stuff that didn't interest me, I opened the front door for Kathryn and followed her out on the front porch. Out of the blue clear sky, she asked, "Can I go with you the next time you and Jack go fishing for crawdads?" I about fell over. Jack and I looked at each other in astonishment. "Did she just ask what I thought she asked?" Jack said. Before I could respond, she asked me again, a little louder this time. "Sure," I said before I had time to think about it. She fired back, "How about tomorrow?" "I didn't think you wanted anything to do with a crawdad," I said. The response was, "I changed my mind after thinking about it." Jack nudged my leg with his head and reminded me that our crawdad hole was our own top secret location, but her persistence had already worn me down, and I agreed to take her anyway.

The next day we were all fired up and ready to go. Jack was feeling a little easier about the situation and started wagging his fluffy white tail at Kathryn as she rode across the front yard and leaned her bike up against a tree. "Can we ride our bikes?" she said excitedly. "Nope," I said. "We have to walk." "You can't ride bikes through fences!"

I grabbed my BB gun and crawdad retrieval gear, and we headed down the gravel road. Jack knew where we were going, so he took the lead about ten feet in front of us while I listened to Kathryn as she did her best to talk my ear off. She covered all of the important stuff like her favorite subjects in school and singing. Now I knew why Jack chose to walk on ahead of us.

We had to cut through a cow pasture to reach our destination, so I got to show Kathryn the proper technique for going through barbed wire fences without tearing your clothes or poking holes in your fingers. She stopped talking long enough to listen to me when she saw all of those sharp, rusty barbs.

After asking me a dozen times about the bull charging us and me telling her that he was a nice bull, we finally went through the fence on the other side of the pasture and arrived at the old crawdad hole. I laid all of my stuff on the thick Bermuda grass and gave Kathryn detailed instructions about tying the raw bacon on the end of her line. After giving her a piece to tie on, she decided that it felt too icky and wanted me to do it for her which I did. When Jack saw that he just rolled his eyes and fell back into the grass, laughing to himself, I'm sure.

The day before, I had cut a limb from a tree in the back yard for Kathryn to use. It was a smaller diameter than mine, so it would have more "action." When the bacon sunk to the bottom, the fun began. Kathryn had a blast. She couldn't believe how hard those mud bugs could jerk on her line.

When we had about twenty or so in the old lard bucket, we decided to call it quits for the day and headed back through the pasture. Kathryn went on ahead with the bucket. She wanted me to see that she could now go through the fence without my assistance. Jack and I brought up the rear with the poles and BB gun. Kathryn was walking along, swinging that bucket from behind her out to the side, when all of a sudden, I got this great idea. Jack told me not to do it, but having full confidence in my ability as a professional shootist, I began to shoot the old bucket on Kathryn's back swing. "Ping, ping, ping," the BB's bounced off the tin bucket, music to my ears.

Of course, this irritated Kathryn to no end as she yelled out "stop it," over and over again. I, however, was not deterred and decided to fire off one more round before we got to the road. I should have listened to the dog. Yep, just as I was pulling the trigger on my last shot, I stepped on a cow patty and slid sideways, sending that little copper BB about two inches off course and smashing directly into her right rear pocket. It was a direct hit to the beautocks.

Kathryn belted out a screechy scream so loud Jack and I both froze in our tracks. My first thought was, "Oh no, I've killed her." My second thought was, "I hope my Mama didn't hear that." Kathryn kept it up and was totally over exaggerating this pain thing. After all, I had been shot several times myself by my cousins, and it didn't hurt all that much. Of course, we were at a much further distance from each other so maybe she did have a point.

After the screaming stopped and she settled down a little, we resumed walking home as Kathryn kept rubbing her rear end and calling me names that I had not heard before. Jack was really embarrassed and didn't want to be associated with me. He was hanging his head in disgust as we approached the house. I kept telling her how sorry I was, but she seemed reluctant to believe me. When we got to my house, Kathryn hopped on her bike, gave me one more icy stare and headed for home.

We put our gear up and put the remainder of the crawdads that we found on the ground in some water. We only had about six now because Kathryn threw the bucket at me and they went all over the pasture. I was just starting to open the screen door on the back porch, when I heard the telephone ring. This was not a good thing.

After the trauma of the day, that telephone was the last thing I wanted to hear. Fear went through my body like the time I licked my finger and stuck it in the light socket because Grandpa told me to. Then, somewhat hysterically, I heard my Mom say, "He did what!" It had just hit the fan. I was toast. *Adios*. After a few more agitated words on the phone, she hung up.

I could hear her coming across the wooden floor at a pretty good clip. She really didn't have to say anything, although she said plenty. I knew the drill. That no good Kathryn went home and shot her mouth off, and once again, I found myself in my own back yard, cutting my own switch for my own mother to beat me with.

It says in the Bible that parents should never whip their children when they are angry, but Mom tore that page out. And this concludes my first and last date with Kathryn.

Seven for a Dollar

We had several little hamburger joints in town and a couple of them even had car hops. These were girls who actually came out to your car and wrote down your food order on a small pad and turned it into the fry cook. When the food was ready, she would bring it out on an adjustable tray and hang it on the driver's window. When your meal was finished, you would turn the car lights on and off a couple of times as a signal for the waitress to come out and pick up the tray. Tips were appreciated.

My favorite place to go was just a couple of miles from our house called the Chicken Coop. It was a tiny place with a wraparound bar and six stools with red seats that swiveled around. On the other side of the bar, was the grill for burgers and a deep fryer for the fresh, crinkle cut fries. Mr. Shannon was the owner. He ran the place by himself and took pride in grinding his meat fresh daily and cutting up his own potatoes. There was no need for a menu. It was hamburgers, fries and pop. He had a wooden rack for candy by the front window, mostly small, individually wrapped pieces that he sold for a penny each.

If you wanted food to go, you could get five hamburgers for a dollar except on Fridays when the special deal was seven hamburgers for a dollar. My Dad would stop in on his way home from work and pick up a sack full every once in a while. They were individually wrapped with thin sheets of white paper and stuffed into a brown paper sack, right off the grill and still hot. By the time he got home, the paper sack was blotched with grease spots and smelled just wonderful. Loaded with chopped white onions and sliced dill pickles, they were very tasty.

On my way home from school sometimes, I would stop in just to say "Hi" and listen to a story or two from Mr. Shannon. He was a soft spoken, interesting man, rather tall and lean, with his shaved head he reminded me of Mr. Clean. He wouldn't say much unless he got to know you and then he would open up and talk a bit.

He was getting up in years and one day he told me he was going to retire. I asked him if he was selling his business, and he said that he had too many good memories there to let someone else take it over. When he quit, he had the building demolished and hauled off. I don't remember what happened to him after that, but I sure did miss Mr. Shannon and the Chicken Coop, oh yeah, and the burger in a basket for twenty-five cents.

Blowin' Stuff Up

W hen I was in elementary school, the local grocery store would pay for empty pop bottles, two cents for the regular size and three cents for the big ones. If you bought a whole case of pop, the bottles came in a wooden crate that was nearly indestructible. We had a large back porch and that's where I would store the empties in one of those crates. When it was filled up, I would sell'um and get cash for recreational purposes.

I usually walked to Wilson elementary school and always kept a look out for discarded bottles in the ditches. Yep, we had litter bugs back then too. People threw trash out their car windows and never gave it a second thought. It was glass containers, metal cans, paper and cigarette butts. We didn't have plastic or Styrofoam.

One Christmas morning, my Mom and Dad surprised me with a new Schwinn bicycle. It had lights, a push button horn and a leather seat. What a machine! I could now travel further, faster and in style.

Our livestock feed came in big burlap sacks that would be used for hauling anything you could stuff in them. I tied one to my handlebars to transport empty pop bottles, but it was a bit awkward and difficult to steer if I had more than nine or ten.

The hardware store downtown carried a few bicycle accessories, one of which was a rectangular shaped, galvanized, wire basket that bolted onto the handle bars. I had to have that, so I saved up the $2.95 and bought it. Problem solved. Now I could ride perfectly balanced with a big load. Got it made in the shade.

With my new basket installed, I could haul about 20 bottles, and when I had collected enough, I would make a run to a little grocery store just off old highway 75. Occasionally, I would have to make more than one trip, so the cashier would set the bottles aside until my deliveries were complete and then pay me from the cash register. After cashing in, I was often tempted to buy the candy bars on the store shelves. They were twice the size of the ones we have today and sold for a whopping 5 cents. Occasionally, I would go ahead and splurge on one of those big, fat "Paydays" all covered with crunchy peanuts. Man, what a treat. They also stocked orange wax whistles. You could blow on one side and they would play about 8 different notes. When tired of blowing on the whistle, you could bite off a chunk and chew it like gum. Ingenious.

The butcher and I were buddies, and he would wrap up some meat scraps for me to give to my dog. Jack could smell the aroma when I approached the house. He would sit real pretty for me as he gobbled up the pieces of freshly cut beef from the white paper sack. Yummy.

Not far from the grocery store was my favorite establishment for my "must have" items, BB's and firecrackers. It was called Bell Salvage. Yep, a multi-purpose, family owned business dealing not only in used car parts, but fireworks and ammo. Who could ask for more?

It was a small operation with a few wrecked cars and trucks neatly parked in rows in the back of the corner lot. The front of the business was previously a gas station with a covered area for refueling and a front door leading to the office on the left adjoining an asphalt floored, dimly lit room complete with a glass enclosed counter that contained the stuff I needed. It was also Mr. Bell, Senior's domain. Mr. Bell, Junior usually worked in the back dismantling cars so the parts could be sold to anyone who needed a bargain. He was always smiling and friendly and seemed to love having his dad around.

Entering that front door was like stepping into another world. Mr. Bell sat close to the entrance in an old wooden chair. He was a short, stout man dressed in pressed trousers and starched shirt buttoned to the top. A brown Stetson hat was on his head and on his feet were old leather shoes that had seen better days. He reminded me of my Grandpa. They were both men of few words.

The air was hazy with thick, white smoke coming from Mr. Bell's ever present hand rolled cigars. You could almost taste the smell of old oily car engines and kerosene used to clean the parts. On windy days, the pine framed structure would creak under the pressure and you thought the place would collapse at any minute, but it never did.

Mr. Bell would stand to his feet and walk over behind the counter when I entered the front door. He knew what I was after. I was probably their most frequent customer, although my pop bottle money wouldn't buy a lot. I picked out my weekly ration of ammo and firecrackers and he told me how much I owed him. That's about all he said. Not "good mornin," "good-bye," "kiss my foot" or anything else, just not much of a conversationalist, that's all.

Regular firecrackers were great, but for more money you could kick it up a notch and go for the M80's, the absolute ultimate in explosive power. They were about as big around as your thumb and close to one and a half inches long with a thick waterproof fuse sticking out of the side. These little babies would explode under water! They could also blow a coffee can up in the air nearly out of sight and even tear a barn door off its hinges. I know about the barn door for a fact and got a deluxe whipping for it too. Eventually, the government decided the citizens were having way too much fun with these and banned them from being manufactured. Not to be deterred, I just learned how to make my own. But that's another story.

Enter the Fat Man

I recall a certain Christmas Eve at the grandparents particularly well. My brother, Jim, was seven years older than me, but my cousins, Steve and Rod, were close to my age and we all got a kick out of the whole Santa Claus thing. Uncle J.B. decided he would do something special for us boys and surprise us with a visit from the old fat man himself. Aunt Dixie made a Santa suit for him out of bright red and white material complete with a wide black belt and a cute little stocking hat with the appropriate white fuzzy ball on the tip. She completed the costume with a long white curly beard that clipped over his ears. There was no need to add any padding for a big belly, J.B. already had that covered.

About half-way into the gift exchanging festivities, Uncle J.B. got up and went to pee but didn't return. Slipping out the back door into the darkness, he made his way to his Buick parked at the far end of the driveway. He then proceeded to take his clothes off and retrieve his costume from the trunk of the car. The finishing touch was a big red sack over his shoulder filled with candy and the like. He looked good. Now it was time for the grand entrance through the front door.

Old George, Grandpa's oversized hound dog, was normally a docile creature, usually always friendly and kept pretty much to himself, spending most of his time stretched out on an old quilt on the front porch. As my uncle crossed the yard humming happy Christmas tunes, he approached the front porch and beheld the dog with his hair standing straight up on his back. George was up on his tippy toes starring into the eyes of the fat man. He was making guttural noises and showing off his front teeth. An unknown intruder had dared to enter his personal domain.

Uncle J.B. was a big strong guy and feared neither man nor beast. As he bent down and extended his hand for the dog to smell, he kept telling old George that he was a "good boy." Taking all of that into consideration, George attacked with fervor knocking Santa to the ground and commenced to tear him a new one.

Pieces of Santa's suit covered the front porch as my uncle made it to his feet with a hundred pounds of hostile animal on his back yelling, "Somebody shoot this thang." I'm sure the neighbors could hear the profanity as we helped Santa Claus through the front door, torn to shreds. Grandpa went out to calm George down. We kids were terrified not only about Santa being wounded, but because he looked like J.B.

Some wanted to blame old George, but after the dust settled and Grandma got my uncle patched up, we realized that he was just doing his job, protecting the family. It wasn't long before the jokes started coming. My uncle got a nickname I can't repeat and everyone was laughing about the whole incident. Don't mess with old George. I don't care who you are.

Wheeler Dealer

Dad was coming home from work one day and stopped to talk to a neighbor who lived down the road. The man had a son who was about my age, twelve or thirteen, I don't remember exactly. As the conversation unfolded the fellow told my Dad that he bought his son a new Honda 90 motorcycle, and his son proceeded to disassemble the bike completely one Saturday while he was at work. Why did he do that? Who knows? Dad wanted to have a look at it, so the neighbor showed him a large cardboard box in his garage with a motorcycle inside in about a thousand pieces! The dealership wouldn't put it back together, and nobody else wanted to tackle the job. It had been in his garage for several months and when my Dad offered the guy 20 bucks for it, he accepted the offer. Twenty bucks for a basket case motorcycle? What would one do with such a mess? The wheels in Dad's mind were turning, and he saw the box of nuts, bolts, fenders and such as, "a piece of cake."

Dad loaded the box in the bed of his 1952 Chevy pickup, brought it home and dumped the contents out on the floor of his shop. When he was home from his regular job, Dad was always working on a project. If someone had a problem with their automobile, he was always happy to make the repair, always free of charge. His brothers, Carl and J.B. thought the same way. They helped many people who were in need and always, for no charge. I never saw Dad work on a motorcycle before, but he seemed to know what he was doing as he worked on the reassembly a little every day.

About two months passed and after walking home from school, I went into the house, dumped my books on the bed and put on my grubby clothes. I proceeded to the back yard and beheld a brand new looking, baby blue, Honda 90 motorcycle! Yep, he did it, and I had a new mode of transportation.

That was one sweet motorcycle and much faster than my bicycle. I eventually sold it for a huge profit and bought a Triumph 250 Tiger Cub. It wouldn't start, but after a little tinkering, it was running like a charm. It was also very quick. I made the mistake of letting a kid ride it, and he slid it into a stop sign and bent the frame. His dad paid me for it. I then purchased a Kawasaki 900 three cylinder. This thing was a rocket, and I could barely hold it up standing on my tiptoes. It was very heavy and too tall for me. I sold it to a guy with long legs.

I was actually making money buying and selling motorcycles that just needed a little work. I eventually bought several cars, fixed them up a bit and sold them for a profit. I did this until I was in my early 20's and paid for my education with my earnings.

I had a couple of early 50's Chevy pickups. In order to start them, you had to flip a switch on the dash to "on" and then press on the starter button with your foot, which was located next to the gas pedal, so you could give it a little gas as the engine was cranking, if you needed to. If the weather was cold, you pulled out a "choke lever" on the dash to give an extra boost from the carburetor. After a few cranks, the engine would fire up and you were ready to roll. These trucks had wooden bed floors and bucked like a mule on a rough road if there was no cargo in the bed. The engine was a straight six cylinder with a three speed manual transmission. There was lots of room under the hood which made them really easy to work on.

One year in particular, I was able to purchase and sell three vehicles. The first one was a sweet little 1954 Dodge with a Hemi engine. The transmission was shifted into gear by a block of little push buttons located on the front of the dashboard by the steering column. It was a solid old car and just needed a tune up, new seat covers and some work on the exhaust. The muffler had a hole in it and was a bit loud. I didn't want to buy a new one so I patched the hole with some heat resistant sealant and covered it with a piece of tin. I covered the tin with more sealant and there you go, good as new.

I sold the Dodge and found a 1956 Plymouth. A little old lady had it parked in her front yard with "for sale" painted on the windshield with white shoe polish. The interior had a fragrance of "White Shoulders" and was in good condition except for the headliner which was easy to replace. The tires were weather cracked, and the wheels had a little rust on them, but nothing a little elbow grease and paint couldn't fix. The engine ran like a sewing machine, and the car was fun to drive. When it was all fixed up, I didn't want to get rid of it, but a fellow at the hardware store offered me three times what I paid for it, so I let her go.

A few weeks later, a friend of the family was buying a new car and offered to sell his used one to me. I rode my motorcycle over to his house to check it out. It was a 1957 green, two door Cadillac in remarkably good condition. The engine was huge and liked to consume large quantities of high octane gasoline. At 30 cents a gallon, it cost a lot to fill that baby up, but man what a ride. It was like sitting in your recliner going down the highway. The suspension, however, was more akin to a pontoon boat.

The guy made me a good deal, so I bought it and drove it for a few months. All I needed to do was clean it up a little bit and wax the exterior. This was another one that was difficult for me to let go of. Looking back now, I wish I had kept them all. Old cars and trucks are just cool, and that's all there is to it.

CPSIA information can be obtained
at www.ICGtesting.com
Printed in the USA
BVHW081106110319
542311BV00013B/514/P

9 781950 034048